Hey, junior detectives! Sergeant Sally will need some help solving the mystery at the aquarium. Pop out your Nightlight Detective paper flashlight and bring clues to light as you read along. Just slip your flashlight under each plastic page and move it around until you find the clue, **in red type**, on each opposite page.

Then keep your paper flashlight in the pocket inside the front cover. (An extra one is included.) Ready? Let's crack the case!

MYSTERY AT THE AQUARIUM

By Karen Kaufman Orloff

Illustrations by Jamie Smith

PETER PAUPER PRESS, INC.
White Plains, New York

The Fishy Friends Aquarium was just about ready to close for the evening when Fred the fish feeder noticed something was not right at the Shipwreck Exhibit.

"Someone has tampered with the treasure chest!" he cried, climbing out of the water. "Gold coins are all over the tank floor. And the strand of pearls is missing!"

"How peculiar," said Miss Megan, the manager, who ran the aquarium. "Who could have gone into the water, and how could they take the pearls?"

"I don't know," said Fred. "But could it have something to do with the penguin I saw escaping from the Penguin Pavilion this afternoon? Did Security find the missing penguin?"

"Not yet, I'm afraid," said Miss Megan. "A penguin on the loose and now a missing necklace! What a wreck of a day!"

"We need help. What should we do?" asked Fred, frazzled.

"This is a case for Sergeant Sally," declared Miss Megan.

"You say a penguin has escaped from the Penguin Pavilion?" asked Sergeant Sally, taking out her notebook. "How many penguins do you keep here at the Pavilion?"

"There are seven penguins in all," Miss Megan told her.

"Aha!" said Sergeant Sally. "I am counting the penguins. There are still seven penguins here. Therefore, I surmise that what you saw was NOT a penguin, but someone who looked like a penguin."

She made a few notes and continued her observations.

"There are several other clues. I noticed small wheel tracks in the sand by the Shipwreck Exhibit. There are also some ticket stubs on the floor. That is highly suspicious. We must gather the suspects. Miss Megan, please summon everyone who works late in the day. Let's meet in front of the shark tank, in the center of the aquarium."

Sergeant Sally looked at all the people gathered in front of the shark tank. There was Bobby, the sea lion trainer; Susie, the clerk at the souvenir shop; Mike, the tour guide; Maisy, the ticket taker; and Mr. Alfred, the host of the aquarium's restaurant.

"I've brought you all here tonight because a serious crime has been committed," said Sergeant Sally. "There is a treasure thief at the aquarium and that is no fish tale! I will figure out who it is or my name isn't Sergeant Sally, and Sergeant Sally always gets her man! Now please follow me to the scene of the crime: the Shipwreck Exhibit."

Sergeant Sally dove into the Shipwreck Exhibit tank and surfaced with a handful of gold coins. "These aren't heavy enough to be real gold coins!" she said. "Are they chocolate?" She chomped on one.

"Plastic, actually," said Miss Megan. "And the pearls are glass."

Sergeant Sally spat out the coin.

"They may be glass," added Fred the Fish Feeder, "but they're the centerpiece of the exhibit! It's not the same without them."

Sally scribbled some things on her notepad. "That is strange. Why would someone steal glass pearls? Perhaps the first clue will give us a hint. Fred thought he saw a penguin escaping. But all the penguins are accounted for. I have therefore concluded that what Fred saw was NOT a penguin but someone dressed like one. Can you help me, NIGHTLIGHT DETECTIVE? Find the person who looks like a penguin."

"You, sir, are wearing a suit that makes you look a lot like a penguin," said Sergeant Sally to Mr. Alfred, the restaurant's host.

"I beg your pardon, Madam, but this is a very fancy tuxedo," retorted Mr. Alfred. "It is certainly NOT a penguin suit!"

"You could have fooled me," said Sergeant Sally. "Still, tell me: Do you like jewelry, specifically pearls?"

"Are you saying I'd wear pearls?" asked Alfred. "Absurd!"

"Well, they would go very nicely with your tux," said Sergeant Sally. "But I suppose it is unlikely. We should concentrate on the next clue—the wheel tracks in the sand. Perhaps the escaped penguin was NOT a person dressed as a penguin after all, but something else. Something with little wheels. **Please help me find something with small wheels, NIGHTLIGHT DETECTIVE!"**

Sergeant Sally and Miss Megan stopped in front of the Sea Lion Stadium. "This cart has small wheels," remarked Sergeant Sally to Bobby, the sea lion trainer. "The wheels seem to fit the tracks made in the sand, near the scene of the crime. How do you explain that?"

"I don't know," said Bobby. "I use this cart to bring food to the sea lions. But as you can see, one of the wheels has come off, so I have not been able to use it in several days."

Sergeant Sally made a note. "So, you are saying this could not have made the tracks near the Shipwreck Exhibit?"

"Yes," said Bobby.

"ARK ARK ARK!" agreed one of the sea lions.

"Well," said Sergeant Sally, "perhaps we should look for something with wheels that looks like a penguin. NIGHTLIGHT DETECTIVE, help me find a penguin on wheels."

"Susie, do you run the Souvenir Shop?" asked Sergeant Sally.

"Yes, ma'am," said Susie.

"I see you sell waterproof remote control plastic penguins that roll on wheels. The wheels are the exact size of the tracks made in the sand! Coincidence? I think not!"

"But they aren't *my* penguins," objected Susie. "I just sell them!"

"That may be so," said Sergeant Sally. "My question is: Could a person operate this toy to pick something up?"

"Probably," said Susie.

"Interesting," said Sergeant Sally. "There is yet another clue. The thief left ripped-up ticket stubs at the scene. This tells us that the thief had a ticket to the aquarium, AND the thief is a bit untidy."

"But why would the thief need several tickets?" asked Miss Megan. "You need only one ticket to get into the aquarium."

"Very observant," said Sergeant Sally. "Who might have a large supply of tickets? Someone who works at the ticket booth? **NIGHTLIGHT DETECTIVE, find the ticket taker!**"

"Maisy, you say you are the ticket taker. What exactly do you do here at the aquarium?" asked Sergeant Sally.

"I take tickets," said Maisy.

"Did you also take the necklace?" asked Sergeant Sally.

"No!" exclaimed Maisy. "Why would I take the necklace?"

"My detective instincts tell me you are not lying," said Sergeant Sally. "Besides, there is no necklace here. There are, however, a lot of tickets. Does anyone else work here at the ticket booth?"

"Yes," said Miss Megan. "Mike the tour guide starts his tours every day at this booth. He always carries a lot of tickets."

Sergeant Sally made more notes. "Where is Mike anyway?"

"He's gone!" said Miss Megan.

"And he left a trail of tickets!" said Sergeant Sally. **"Follow the tickets to find Mike, NIGHTLIGHT DETECTIVE!"**

"Why, look at all these blue tickets!" shouted Sergeant Sally. "They are leading us to the Rainforest Exhibit. We'd better hurry!"

"Better hurry! Better hurry!" squawked a parrot on a perch.

"Which way did Mike go?" asked Miss Megan, forgetting for a moment that the parrot was just a bird.

"Better hurry!" repeated the bird. "Have a cracker?"

"No time for crackers!" replied Sergeant Sally. "I believe we are on Mike's trail. NIGHTLIGHT DETECTIVE, help me find Mike, the tour guide!"

"Mike is somewhere close by," whispered Sergeant Sally, staring at the monkeys. One of them, chewing on a blue ticket stub, stared back.

"But it's such a jungle in here," said Miss Megan. "However will we spot Mike?"

"Do not worry, Miss Megan," said Sergeant Sally. "The Nightlight Detective will assist us. NIGHTLIGHT DETECTIVE, help me track down Mike, the tour guide."

Sergeant Sally and the others looked up. Mike, the tour guide, was perched high on a branch, covered in monkeys.

"What are you doing up there? Come down, in the name of the law!" demanded Sergeant Sally.

"I confess! I took the necklace! Just get me away from these monkeys!" shouted Mike.

"Aha!" cried Sergeant Sally. "I knew there was something fishy about you. Give me the necklace this instant."

"I don't have it," said Mike, clinging to the tree trunk.

"Miss Megan, please ask the monkey keepers to help get Mike down," said Sergeant Sally. **"My NIGHTLIGHT DETECTIVE FRIEND will help me find the necklace!"**

"I had no idea octopi liked pearls!" cried Sergeant Sally. "Can you explain this, Mike?"

Mike hung his head. "Maisy and I were playing with a remote control penguin by the Shipwreck Exhibit. She bet me I couldn't pick up the pearls in the tank with it."

"I didn't think you'd actually do it!" Maisy exclaimed.

"I managed to pull the pearls out of the water with the penguin," Mike continued, "but just then we heard Fred the fish feeder coming! We panicked and ran away. I didn't know what to do with the pearls, so I put them in with the octopus for safekeeping. "

"We were going to return them after everyone went home tonight," added Maisy.

Miss Megan shook her head. "Well, that's a whale of a tale," she said. "You're going to have to make up for the trouble you've caused. Since you stashed the pearls with the octopus, you'll be in charge of cleaning its tank from now on. Octopi can be mischievous, but I think you're up to the challenge."

"This has been a fine kettle of fish," said Sergeant Sally, shutting her notepad. "But as everyone knows, I always get my man! **Thank *you*, NIGHTLIGHT DETECTIVE!**"

For Max, who loves Sergeant Sally
–KKO

For Mum, Dad, and Guinness (the dog)
–JS

PETER PAUPER PRESS

OUR COMPANY

In 1928, at the age of twenty-two, Peter Beilenson began printing books on a small press in the basement of his parents' home in Larchmont, New York. Peter—and later, his wife, Edna—sought to create fine books that sold at "prices even a pauper could afford."

Today, still family owned and operated, Peter Pauper Press continues to honor our founders' legacy of quality, value, and fun for big kids and small kids alike.

Illustrations copyright © 2014 Jamie Smith
Designed by Heather Zschock

Copyright © 2014
Peter Pauper Press, Inc.
Manufactured for Peter Pauper Press, Inc.
202 Mamaroneck Avenue,
White Plains, NY 10601
All rights reserved
ISBN 978-1-4413-1615-8
Printed in China

Published in the United Kingdom and Europe by
Peter Pauper Press Inc. c/o White Pebble International
Unit 2, Plot 11 Terminus Road
Chichester, West Sussex PO19 8TX, UK
7 6 5 4 3 2 1

Visit us at www.peterpauper.com